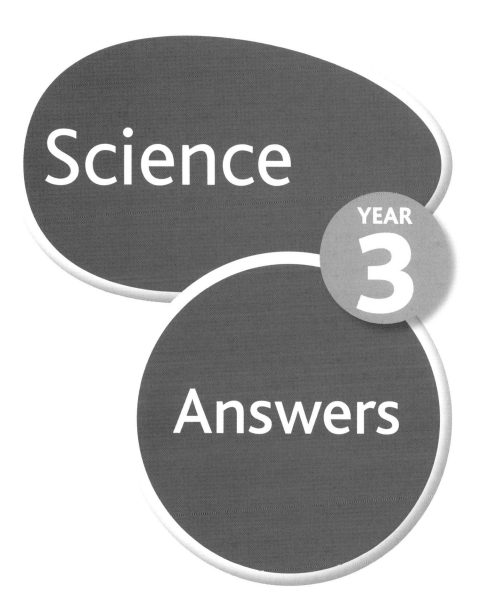

Science

YEAR 3

Answers

Sue Hunter

Jenny Macdonald

GALORE PARK

AN HACHETTE UK COMPANY

About the authors

Sue Hunter has been a science teacher in a variety of schools for more years than she cares to remember. Her experiences have included teaching in a choir school and a local authority middle school, teaching GCSE and A level in the Netherlands and a short spell as a full-time mother of two. She was Head of Science at St Hugh's School in Oxfordshire until her recent retirement and is a member of the Common Entrance setting team. She has run a number of training courses for prep school teachers, including at Malvern College and for the Independent Association of Preparatory Schools (IAPS), and is currently IAPS Subject Leader for science and a member of the Independent Schools Inspectorate. She has also served for a number of years as a governor of local primary schools.

Jenny Macdonald has been a teacher for many years, teaching in both state and private schools. For the last 15 years she has been teaching science at St Hugh's School in Oxfordshire. She moved to Oxfordshire in the 1970s and has always enjoyed outdoor pursuits, having raised three children and countless chickens, sheep and dogs on the family smallholding. She is chairman of a local choral society, sings in a variety of local choirs, and would like to have more time to relax in the chairs that she enjoys re-upholstering.

Every effort has been made to trace all copyright holders, but if any have been inadvertently overlooked, the Publishers will be pleased to make the necessary arrangements at the first opportunity.

Although every effort has been made to ensure that website addresses are correct at time of going to press, Galore Park cannot be held responsible for the content of any website mentioned in this book. It is sometimes possible to find a relocated web page by typing in the address of the home page for a website in the URL window of your browser.

Hachette UK's policy is to use papers that are natural, renewable and recyclable products and made from wood grown in sustainable forests. The logging and manufacturing processes are expected to conform to the environmental regulations of the country of origin.

Orders: please contact Bookpoint Ltd, 130 Milton Park, Abingdon, Oxon OX14 4SB. Telephone: (44) 01235 827720. Fax: (44) 01235 400454. Email education@bookpoint.co.uk Lines are open from 9 a.m. to 5 p.m., Monday to Saturday, with a 24-hour message answering service. Visit our website at www.galorepark.co.uk for details of revision guides for Common Entrance, examination papers and Galore Park publications.

ISBN: 978 1 4718 5629 7

© Sue Hunter and Jenny Macdonald 2015

First published in 2015 by

Galore Park Publishing Ltd,

An Hachette UK Company

Carmelite House

50 Victoria Embankment

London EC4Y 0DZ

www.galorepark.co.uk

Impression number   10 9 8 7 6 5 4 3 2 1

Year   2019 2018 2017 2016 2015

Typeset in India by Aptara Inc.

Printed in the UK

A catalogue record for this title is available from the British Library.

Contents

Introduction

About this book

Science is a subject that invites enquiry. The text in *Science Year 3* contains many interesting facts and opens the way for further research should a child feel inclined to find out more. Each chapter includes a number of exercises that are designed to focus the readers' attention on what they have read, assess their understanding of the material and encourage them to think more analytically about the topic. There are a number of different types of exercise, for example cloze ('fill in the gaps') exercises, comprehension-type questions and extension exercises requiring thought and application. All can be used in a number of ways depending on the ability of the pupils and the requirements of a lesson. The extension exercises, for example, could be used by teachers as stimuli for discussion, homework activities, opportunities for further development for quick workers, and so on.

The answers given here should be seen as a guide. We do not expect every child to reproduce our answers exactly and each child should be encouraged to respond to the best of their ability. For some, success will be achieved if they can correctly extract basic information from the text. Others can be encouraged to look for more than the most basic answer by reading the text more critically. Those with the ability and interest can be encouraged to find out more and expand their knowledge through further reading or to think more deeply about the implications and applications of the material offered.

Sue Hunter and Jenny Macdonald
August 2015

① Life processes

This chapter covers the following elements of the National Curriculum for Year 3.

Pupils should be taught to:

● explore and compare the differences between things that are living, dead, and things that have never been alive (Y2).

It also includes the following elements not mentioned in the National Curriculum but included in the ISEB syllabus for Year 3 (ISEB 1a and 1b):

● the distinction between living and non-living things
● that living things all carry out life processes
● that the life processes common to humans and other animals include nutrition, movement, growth and reproduction
● that life processes are common to both plants and animals
● that the life processes common to plants include growth, nutrition and reproduction.

Activities in this chapter offer opportunities to work scientifically by:

● making systematic and careful observations
● identifying differences, similarities or changes related to simple scientific ideas and processes.

Exercise 1.1a

1 life processes

2 food, nutrition

3 larger, growth

4 reproduction, extinct

5 climbing, running, swimming (in any order), movement

6 flowers, leaves (in either order)

Exercise 1.1b: extension

1 organisms

2 excretion

3 respiration

4 sensing and reacting to what is going on around you

5 The snakes eat warm-blooded animals, such as mice or bats. They are able to detect the warmth of the animals' bodies in the form of infra-red energy using special sense organs on the sides of their heads.

Green plants

This chapter covers the following elements of the National Curriculum for Year 3.

Pupils should be taught to:

- identify and describe the functions of different parts of flowering plants: roots, stem/trunk, leaves and flowers
- explore the requirements of plants for life and growth (air, light, water, nutrients from soil, and room to grow) and how they vary from plant to plant
- investigate the way in which water is transported within plants
- explore the part that flowers play in the life cycle of flowering plants, including pollination, seed formation and seed dispersal.

It also includes the following elements not mentioned in the National Curriculum:

- how to demonstrate the effect of variation in light, temperature and water on plant growth; that air supplies a plant with carbon dioxide for making food; that plants also need oxygen (ISEB 2b)
- that green plants use energy from the Sun to produce food (photosynthesis); about the role of the green pigment (chlorophyll) in the leaf and stem in capturing this light energy (ISEB 2c)
- about basic details of flower structure; the terms *carpel*, *stamen* and *petal* (ISEB 2e)
- experiments to show that water, air and warmth are needed for germination (ISEB 2e).

Activities in this chapter offer opportunities to work scientifically by:

- making systematic and careful observations and, where appropriate, taking accurate measurements using standard units, using a range of equipment
- gathering, recording, classifying and presenting data in a variety of ways to help in answering questions
- recording findings using simple scientific language, drawings, labelled diagrams, bar charts, and tables
- setting up simple practical enquiries, comparative and fair tests.

Exercise 2.1

1 leaf

2 stem

3 flower

4 root

5 root

6 stem

Exercise 2.2a

1 photosynthesis

2 **(a)** chlorophyll

(b) It absorbs light from the Sun. This is the energy source needed for the plant to make its food.

3 Water is taken in from the soil by the roots and then moves up through tubes in the stem to the leaves and other parts of the plant.

4 Carbon dioxide enters through tiny holes (called stomata) in the underside of the leaf.

5 mineral salts

Exercise 2.2b

1 photosynthesis

2 chlorophyll, sunlight

3 soil, roots, stem

4 holes

5 mineral salts

Exercise 2.2c: extension

1 Carbon dioxide is given out by animals and plants as a waste product of respiration. (Accept 'As a result of burning fossil fuels.')

2 oxygen

3 Answers should include some or all of the following ideas: Without sunlight life would not be possible. Plants would not be able to carry out photosynthesis so the food supply for all animals would stop. They would also not produce oxygen so respiration would not be possible and animals would suffocate. It would also become too cold for life to continue.

Exercise 2.3a

1 the stamen

2 the carpel

3 the transfer of pollen from one flower to another flower (of the same type)

4 brightly coloured petals and nectar (also accept scent)

5 The insect visits one flower, pushing past the stamens to reach the nectar. Pollen brushes off onto the insect's body. The insect then flies to another flower and the pollen is brushed off onto the sticky tip of the carpel.

6 small green flowers, possibly dangling in the wind

7 The pollen grain burrows down through the carpel to join with the egg. The egg then becomes a seed. The petals and stamens fall off and the carpel becomes a fruit or seed case.

Exercise 2.3b

1 stamen – makes pollen
petal – attracts insects
carpel – contains eggs

2 (a) To make a seed, a grain of **pollen** must join with an **egg**.

(b) Pollen can be moved from one flower to another by an **insect** or by the **wind**. This process is called **pollination**.

(c) After pollination the eggs turn into **seeds**.

Exercise 2.4a

1 Spreading seeds away from the parent plant to grow in new places.

2 Seeds are dispersed to prevent the seedlings having to compete with each other and with the parent plant for water and light.

3 The dandelion's seed case has a parachute, which is blown by the wind, keeping the seed in the air for a long time so it can travel further.

4 Juicy fruits attract birds and other animals, which eat the fruit. The seeds are then dispersed in the droppings.

5 Squirrels bury acorns as a store of food for the winter. Some of the acorns get forgotten and may grow into new plants.

Exercise 2.4b: extension

1 Answers should suggest a possible dispersal method and give a reason for the choice. Give credit for sensible suggestions supported by good reasons even if they are incorrect.
Burdock – hitches a ride on the fur of an animal; the seed case has little hooks on it.
Elm – wind; the seed is in the middle of a 'wing' which will catch the wind.
Pomegranate – animals will eat the fruitlets and the seed will be dispersed in the droppings; the seeds are surrounded by juicy fruit.
Horse chestnut – buried by animals; the seed has a big food store inside it.

2 The peanut plant buries its own seed. When the flower has been pollinated and the pollen and egg have joined together, the petals fall off and the stem of the flower grows downwards towards the soil. The tip of the flower stem is pushed down into the soil and the seed forms inside a woody husk under the soil.

Exercise 2.5

1 Germination is when a seed begins to grow a root, the first stage in growing a new plant.

2 The baby plant needs energy to grow its first root and shoot because it cannot make its own food until the leaves grow.

3 The seed needs water and oxygen from the air. It also needs to be warm enough.

4 The root grows first to anchor the plant into the ground, to take in water and to take in mineral salts from the soil.

A healthy diet

This chapter covers the following elements of the National Curriculum for Year 3.

Pupils should be taught to:

- identify that animals, including humans, need the right types and amount of nutrition, and that they cannot make their own food; they get nutrition from what they eat.

It also includes the following elements not mentioned in the National Curriculum:

1 the names and positions of the following related organs: brain, heart, lungs, stomach, intestines (ISEB Y3 3a)
2 about the value of a balanced diet, composed of carbohydrates, fats, proteins, vitamins, mineral salts, fibre and water, in the maintenance of good health (ISEB Y3 3b)
3 examples of foods which are rich in carbohydrates and proteins; vitamin C is an example of a vitamin, and calcium salts are an example of a mineral; the effects on humans of lack of vitamin C and calcium; the dangers of an excessive intake of animal fats; one good source of each food component (ISEB Y3 3c).

Activities in this chapter offer opportunities to work scientifically by:

- making systematic and careful observations and, where appropriate, taking accurate measurements
- identifying differences, similarities or changes related to simple scientific ideas and processes
- gathering, recording, classifying and presenting data in a variety of ways to help in answering questions.

Exercise 3.1

1 organs

2 cells

3 oxygen, carbon dioxide

4 stomach

5 heart, oxygen, food

Exercise 3.2a

1 a diet including all the nutrients, water and fibre we need in the right quantities to keep us healthy

2 carbohydrates (starchy/sugary) and fats

3 proteins

4 Fat is stored under the skin, keeping us warm and providing a store of energy.

5 Too much fat causes heart disease and makes people obese.

6 Fruit and vegetables provide vitamins, minerals and fibre. They also contain water and sugars.

Exercise 3.2b

1 diet, nutrients (accept energy/vitamins)

2 carbohydrates

3 energy, warm

4 obese

5 grow

6 fibre, vitamins (in either order; accept carbohydrates/energy/nutrients)

Exercise 3.2c: extension

Answers should include information as given in the text. If research is carried out some additional material could be included, for example:

● Proteins – lack of protein will result in poor growth (and weak muscles, weakened immune system; kwashiorkor is a disease in children with severe protein deficiency often resulting in a characteristic 'pot-belly').
● Carbohydrate – lack of carbohydrate will result in extreme tiredness (and can cause hypoglycaemia [low blood sugar] resulting in light-headedness and confusion).
● Fats – lack of fats in the diet reduces the body's insulation and ability to control body temperature. It also reduces the internal store of energy so if you were ill and unable to eat you would have fewer reserves to draw on. (Lack of fat reduces absorption of some vitamins, for example A, D, E and K.)

Exercise 3.3

1 vitamin C

2 twelve, air

3 teeth, black

4 oranges

5 marmalade

6 Australia

Skeleton and movement

This chapter covers the following elements of the National Curriculum for Year 3.

Pupils should be taught to:

● identify that humans and some other animals have skeletons and muscles for support, protection and movement.

It also includes the following elements not mentioned in the National Curriculum:

● that some animals with internal skeletons are called vertebrates (ISEB Y3 3d)
● the location of the skull, backbone (vertebral column), rib cage, pelvis, collarbone and shoulder blade (ISEB Y3 3d)
● what would happen if humans did not have skeletons (ISEB Y3 3e)
● to observe and compare the movement of animals both with and without skeletons (ISEB Y3 3e).

Activities in this chapter offer opportunities to work scientifically by:

● asking relevant questions and using different types of scientific enquiries to answer them
● making systematic and careful observations
● using straightforward scientific evidence to answer questions or to support their findings.

Exercise 4.1a

1 To support the body, protect important organs and provide a framework for muscles to pull on to move the body.

2 the brain

3 the rib cage

4 the heart

5 the place where two or more bones are joined together

6 So that we can move our bodies in lots of different ways.

Exercise 4.1b

1 skeleton

2 heart, lungs (in either order)

3 joints

4 muscles

Exercise 4.2a

1 Animals that have internal skeletons are called **vertebrates**. These animals can move when muscles **pull** on their bones. Animals that do not have internal skeletons are called **invertebrates**. Some of these have a **hard** outer shell around their bodies.

2

vertebrates	invertebrates
eagle	earthworm
human	beetle
horse	snail
kangaroo	
snake	

Exercise 4.2b

1 Answers could include:
   Dolphin has no back legs because this makes it easier for it to swim/more streamlined/it does not walk.
   Dolphin front limbs have long 'fingers' – to support flippers/increase surface area pushing on water.
   Dolphin has smaller skull/longer, more pointed skull – for streamlining in the water/better for catching fish.

2 Larger invertebrates include octopus, (giant) squid, sea cucumbers, crabs, lobsters, giant African snails, giant millipedes, and so on. The largest invertebrate is probably the colossal squid (c. 12 m/450 kg+). The largest land invertebrate is the coconut crab (c. 40 cm long/4 kg).

   The largest invertebrates live in the sea because the water provides support for their bodies. On land, their bodies would collapse due to gravity without support and an exoskeleton is not strong enough to support a large body.

Rocks

This chapter covers the following elements of the National Curriculum for Year 3.

Pupils should be taught to:

- compare and group together different kinds of rocks on the basis of their appearance and simple physical properties
- describe in simple terms how fossils are formed when things that have lived are trapped within rock.

It also includes the following elements not mentioned in the National Curriculum:

- to describe and group rocks on the basis of their characteristics, including appearance, texture and permeability (ISEB Y3 4a)
- how to compare and group together different kinds of rock on the basis of their appearance and simple physical properties; how to use a hand lens to determine whether they contain grains or crystals (ISEB Y3 4a)
- how sedimentary rocks are formed; how to model fossil formation by making plaster casts of shells; understanding that it is usually only the hard parts of organisms which are preserved (ISEB Y3 4c).

Activities in this chapter offer opportunities to work scientifically by:

- asking relevant questions and using different types of scientific enquiries to answer them
- setting up simple practical enquiries, comparative and fair tests
- making systematic and careful observations and, where appropriate, taking accurate measurements using standard units, using a range of equipment
- gathering, recording, classifying and presenting data in a variety of ways to help in answering questions
- recording findings using simple scientific language, drawings, labelled diagrams, bar charts, and tables
- reporting on findings from enquiries, including oral and written explanations, displays or presentations of results and conclusions.

Exercise 5.1

1 crust = the layer of solid rock on the surface of the Earth
   sediment = a mixture of sand, mud and parts of animals and plants that settles at the bottom of a lake or sea
   volcano = a mountain made when liquid rock escapes through a gap in the Earth's crust
   fossil = the remains of a dead animal or plant trapped in the rock millions of years ago

2 (a) Rocks may be made up from **crystals** or **grains**.

 (b) Rocks made from sand, mud and parts of animals and plants are called **sedimentary** rocks.

3 The animal died and its body sank to the bottom of the sea or lake. Layers of sediment built up over the remains. The layers above pressed down and squeezed the lower layer where the animal's remains were. This turned them into rock.

6 Soils

This chapter covers the following elements of the National Curriculum for Year 3.

Pupils should be taught to:

● recognise that soils are made from rocks and organic matter.

It also includes the following elements not mentioned in the National Curriculum:

● to describe and group soils on the basis of their characteristics, including appearance, texture and permeability (ISEB Y3 4a)
● about different kinds of soils, e.g. sand, clay, loam; how particle size affects drainage; the term humus and how this enriches the soil (ISEB Y3 4a)
● how to separate solid particles of different sizes by sieving (e.g. those in soil) (ISEB Y3 4b).

Activities in this chapter offer opportunities to work scientifically by:

● asking relevant questions and using different types of scientific enquiries to answer them
● setting up simple practical enquiries, comparative and fair tests
● making systematic and careful observations and, where appropriate, taking accurate measurements using standard units, using a range of equipment
● gathering, recording, classifying and presenting data in a variety of ways to help in answering questions
● recording findings using simple scientific language, drawings, labelled diagrams, bar charts, and tables
● reporting on findings from enquiries, including oral and written explanations, displays or presentations of results and conclusions.

Exercise 6.1a

1 gravel = rocky pieces more than 2 mm across
   sand = small rocky pieces, smaller than 2 mm but big enough to see
   silt = very tiny rocky pieces
   humus = remains of dead plants and animals

2 Humus holds water in the soil and provides mineral salts.

3 By collecting plant material from the garden and kitchen and putting it in a compost heap. (Accept valid alternative suggestions.)

4 water and air (accept living things)

5 The rock may be broken up by wind, rain and ice. It may fall into a river and be tumbled around and broken down further. It might be left by the side of the river or dropped as sediment when the river floods and become part of the soil.

6 There are bigger spaces between the rocky pieces in the soil for it to drain through.

7 loam

Exercise 6.1b

1 silt, sand, gravel

2 (a) humus

  (b) It holds water in the soil and contains mineral salts.

3 through a soil with big rocky pieces

4 loam

Exercise 6.1c: extension

Field 1 = loam

Field 2 = clay

Field 3 = sandy

Exercise 6.2a

1 invertebrates

2 earthworms, moles (in either order)

3 air, water (in either order), roots

4 leaves, humus

Exercise 6.2b: extension

1 In wet weather the burrow could flood and the worm would drown if it could not get to the surface quickly enough. It will therefore move upwards towards the surface. In hot, sunny weather the soil near the surface may dry out. Worms need to stay moist at all times so they move downwards to the cooler, damper conditions deeper in the soil.

2 Count worm casts early in the morning before they get broken up. It is also possible to bring the worms to the surface by pouring a lot of water onto the grass. They can then be counted before they burrow back down into the soil. (For further information, see http://www.opalexplorenature.org/soilsurvey.)

3 This will need assessing individually and can be used to support literacy targets. Pupils should use the information from the text above and earlier in the chapter to write a short but exciting account of events in an earthworm's day/night.

Light

This chapter covers the following elements of the National Curriculum for Year 3.

Pupils should be taught to:

- recognise that they need light in order to see things and that dark is the absence of light
- notice that light is reflected from surfaces
- recognise that light from the Sun can be dangerous and that there are ways to protect their eyes
- recognise that shadows are formed when the light from a light source is blocked by a solid object
- find patterns in the way that the size of shadows changes.

It also includes the following elements not mentioned in the National Curriculum:

- that a luminous source gives out light; examples of luminous sources; that light travels in straight lines; how to indicate a ray of light like this:

$$\longrightarrow$$

(ISEB Y3 5a)

- the terms *opaque*, *translucent* and *transparent*; how shadows are formed by opaque objects, investigating the effect of different distances between source, object and screen (ISEB Y3 5b)
- that we see things only when light from them enters our eyes
- how we see luminous objects; how to draw simple diagrams to show that light rays, travelling in straight lines, enter the eye(s) directly from the luminous object (ISEB Y3 5d).

Activities in this chapter offer opportunities to work scientifically by:

- setting up simple practical enquiries, comparative and fair tests
- making systematic and careful observations and, where appropriate, taking accurate measurements using standard units, using a range of equipment, including data loggers
- recording findings using simple scientific language, drawings, labelled diagrams, keys, bar charts, and tables
- using results to draw simple conclusions, make predictions for new values, suggest improvements and raise further questions
- identifying differences, similarities or changes related to simple scientific ideas and processes
- using straightforward scientific evidence to answer questions or to support their findings.

Exercise 7.1a

1 Plants need light to carry out photosynthesis to make food.

2 the Sun

3 giving out light

4 No. The Moon reflects light from the Sun to the Earth.

5 (A) star – luminous   (F) candle – luminous

   (B) television – luminous   (G) moon – reflective

   (C) mirror – reflective   (H) desk lamp – luminous

   (D) diamond ring – reflective   (I) firework – luminous

   (E) fluorescent vest – reflective   (J) compact disc – reflective

Exercise 7.1b

1 see   4 reflective

2 food   5 Sun, Moon

3 luminous

Exercise 7.1c: extension

Peter is correct. If there were no light, plants would be unable to carry out photosynthesis. If this were the case there would be no food for us to eat and no oxygen in the air for us to breathe.

Exercise 7.2a

1 Light always travels in **straight** lines.

2 Diagram should show the candle and the face of the boy. A straight line, drawn with a ruler and pencil, should run from the flame of the candle to the eye of the boy. An arrow in the centre of the line should point from the candle to the boy to show the direction of travel of the light.

3 sunglasses and a cap

4 Sunlight is bright enough to cause permanent damage to the eyes.

Exercise 7.2b

1 straight   3 sunglasses, cap

2 eyes   4 Sun

Exercise 7.3a

1 A shadow is formed when an opaque object blocks the light.

2 Transparent materials allow nearly all the light to pass through them and we can see through them clearly. Translucent materials allow some light to pass through but scatter it so that we cannot see through them clearly.

3 opaque

4 By changing the position of the object in relation to the light source and/or screen.

Exercise 7.3b

1 shadow, blocks

2 transparent

3 opaque

4 translucent

5 smaller

Exercise 7.3c: extension

1

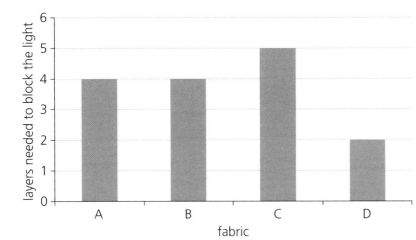

2 (a) fabric D

  (b) This fabric needed two layers to block the light but the others needed more.

Exercise 7.4

Light can bounce back off some surfaces. We call this **reflection**. Surfaces that are **shiny/reflective** are very good at bouncing light.

When we look in a mirror we see a picture that is nearly the same as our real face, but it is **back-to-front**.

⑧ Friction and movement

This chapter covers the following elements of the National Curriculum for Year 3.

Pupils should be taught to:

- compare how things move on different surfaces.

It also includes the following elements not mentioned in the National Curriculum:

- that forces can push or pull on an object (ISEB Y3 6a)
- that all forces are pushes or pulls (ISEB Y3 6a)
- everyday examples of forces in action (ISEB Y3 6a)
- about friction, including air resistance, as a force which slows moving objects and may prevent objects from starting to move (ISEB Y3 6d)
- about the concept of friction as a force which opposes the relative movement of surfaces, with reference to everyday situations (ISEB Y3 6d)
- how to carry out investigations involving friction (ISEB Y3 6d).

Activities in this chapter offer opportunities to work scientifically by:

- asking relevant questions and using different types of scientific enquiries to answer them
- setting up simple practical enquiries, comparative and fair tests
- making systematic and careful observations and, where appropriate, taking accurate measurements using standard units, using a range of equipment
- gathering, recording, classifying and presenting data in a variety of ways to help in answering questions
- recording findings using simple scientific language, drawings, labelled diagrams, keys, bar charts, and tables
- reporting on findings from enquiries, including oral and written explanations, displays or presentations of results and conclusions
- using results to draw simple conclusions, make predictions for new values, suggest improvements and raise further questions
- identifying differences, similarities or changes related to simple scientific ideas and processes
- using straightforward scientific evidence to answer questions or to support their findings.

Exercise 8.1a

1 a push or a pull

2 They change the speed or direction of movement, or change the shape of objects.

3 by two surfaces rubbing together

4 A rough surface causes the most friction.

5 The lumps and bumps on the surfaces get caught up with one another.

6 The grit makes the road surface rougher, making it easier for the cars to grip the road.

Exercise 8.1b

1 push, pull (in either order)

2 speed, shape (in either order)

3 rub

4 rough

5 increases, skidding

Exercise 8.2a

1 for example, between a tyre and the road, on soles of shoes, when gripping something, when rubbing out a pencil mark

2 for example, a door hinge, playground slide, pulling a load across a surface, air resistance on racing cyclist

3 The oil allows the surfaces to move smoothly past one another and prevents wear (and noise).

4 air resistance

5 shaped so that the air (or water) can move smoothly past the object, reducing air resistance

6 They both need to move efficiently through the water so they are both streamlined.

Exercise 8.2b

1 grip

2 useful, nuisance

3 smooth (accept streamlined)

4 oil, grease (in either order)

5 streamlined (accept smooth)

Exercise 8.2c: extension

Sharks' streamlined bodies suggest that they need to swim fast through the water. Puffer fish are not streamlined because they do not swim fast to catch their prey.

Exercise 8.3

1 in Wiltshire

2 about four thousand years ago

3 about 240 miles

4 about 50 tonnes

5 There would be a huge amount of friction between the blocks and the ground because both surfaces are rough and the blocks are so heavy.

6 They were probably placed on rollers made from tree trunks and pulled along using leather ropes. As each roller rolled out at the back, it would be moved to the front.

7 As the block was pulled, the rollers under it would roll across the ground, carrying the block with them. This would reduce the friction between the block and the ground.

8 Some may have been carried on barges along rivers.

9 The larger ones were too heavy to be carried in this way.

10 Stonehenge may have been a temple, a huge sundial or a place to observe the movement of the stars and planets.

9 Magnets

This chapter covers the following elements of the National Curriculum for Year 3.

Pupils should be taught to:

- notice that some forces need contact between two objects, but magnetic forces can act at a distance
- observe how magnets attract or repel each other and attract some materials and not others
- compare and group together a variety of everyday materials on the basis of whether they are attracted to a magnet, and identify some magnetic materials
- describe magnets as having two poles
- predict whether two magnets will attract or repel each other, depending on which poles are facing.

It also includes the following elements not mentioned in the National Curriculum:

- that magnetic materials such as iron and steel are attracted to a magnet (ISEB Y3 6b)
- that a freely suspended bar magnet comes to rest in a north–south direction and acts as a compass (ISEB Y3 6b)
- that magnetic effects will pass through some materials (ISEB Y3 6b)
- how to compare the strengths of two or more magnets (ISEB Y3 6b).

Activities in this chapter offer opportunities to work scientifically by:

- asking relevant questions and using different types of scientific enquiries to answer them
- setting up simple practical enquiries, comparative and fair tests
- making systematic and careful observations
- gathering, recording, classifying and presenting data in a variety of ways to help in answering questions
- recording findings using simple scientific language, drawings, labelled diagrams, bar charts, and tables
- reporting on findings from enquiries, including oral and written explanations, displays or presentations of results and conclusions
- using results to draw simple conclusions, make predictions for new values, suggest improvements and raise further questions
- identifying differences, similarities or changes related to simple scientific ideas and processes
- using straightforward scientific evidence to answer questions or to support their findings.

Exercise 9.1a

1 iron, steel (in either order)

2 magnetic

3 for example: plastic, copper, wood, fabric (or any two other non-magnetic materials)

4 non-magnetic

Exercise 9.1b: extension

1 This could be done by putting paper clips or other small pieces of a magnetic material onto the fish.

2 Individual ideas will need consideration. Designs should show understanding of the fact that the steel cans will be attracted to a magnet but the aluminium ones will not.

Exercise 9.2a

1 Two south-seeking poles of a magnet will **repel** each other.

2 A north-seeking pole will **attract** a south-seeking pole.

3 If you hang a bar magnet up it will point to **north** and **south**.

4 Plastic is non-magnetic so it is **not attracted to** / **unaffected by** a magnet.

Exercise 9.2b: extension

Emily should bring both poles of the magnet towards the end of each block of metal.

The aluminium will be unaffected by the magnet.

The steel will be attracted to both poles.

The magnet will be attracted to one pole and repelled by the other.